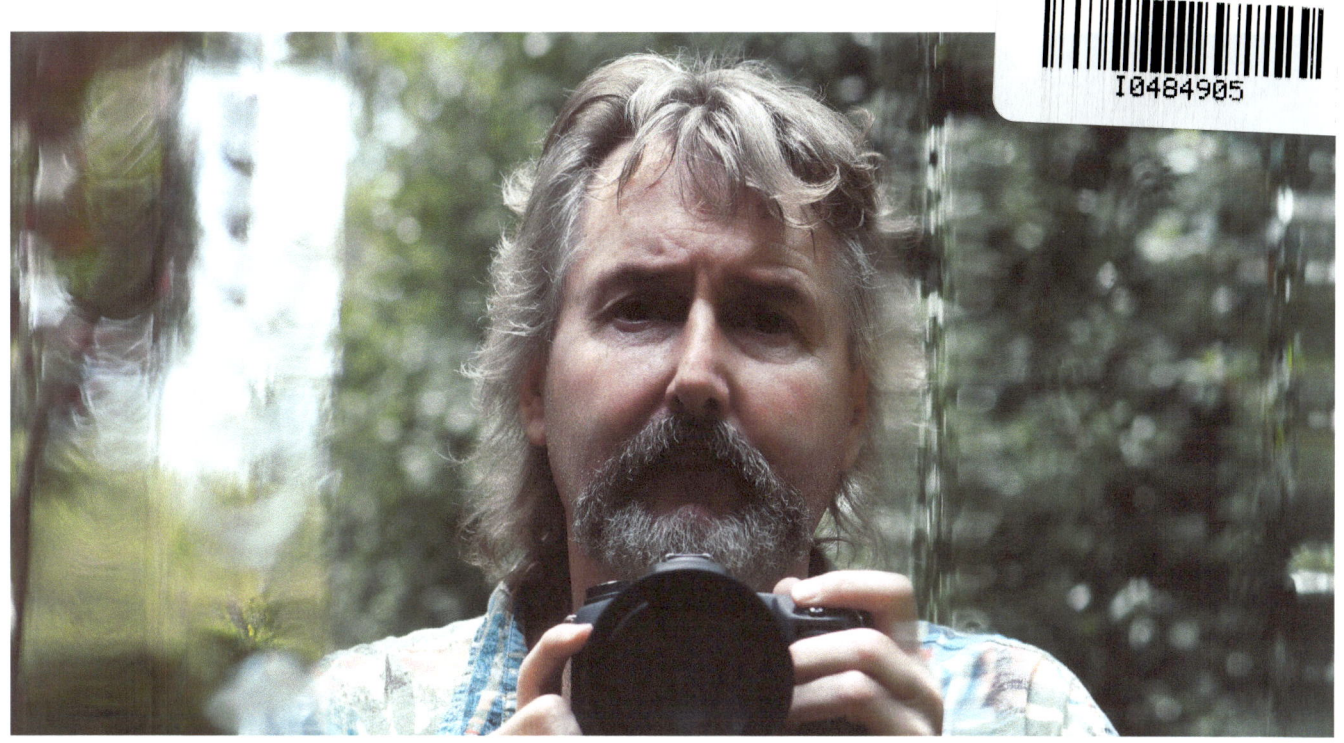

Colorblind Photograph Collection

Decades of being around accomplished artists producing absolutely phenomenal quality work has taught that we are capable of greatness. It is possible to meet our destiny and become it. Experiencing excellence done with such apparent magical ease and humble selfless gratification is the inspiration for this original photography.

Being colorblind gives an advantage when composing black & white... less confusion. This special collection exhibits the lonely freedom of a hidden perspective selected from thousands of captures during years of travels. All images were framed in the camera and presented without edits, genuine as seen through the lens. Panchromatic conversion applied by proprietary process.

Original fine art and custom work available.

info@ BEACHNOISE.com

Joseph Fleming

0125

0351

0354

0437

0705

0780

0826

0920

1085

1088

1581

1608

1976

2068

2180

2397

2467

2686

2962

3147

3151

3359

3656

3714

3720

3916

3937

3943

4035

4070

4099

4193

4533

5492

5541

5705

5708

5750

5784

5811

5844

5846

6095

6176

7182

7409

7656

8079

8173

8249

8345

8407

8449

8470

8471

8889

9024

9353

9430

9970

9975

9980

9998

10002

www.ingramcontent.com/pod-product-compliance
Lightning Source LLC
Chambersburg PA
CBHW050412180526

45159CB00005B/2241